Euphoria

Euphoria

Glimpses of Heart

Susmita Sarkar

EXCELLER BOOKS®
A GLOBAL PRESS

Euphoria

Glimpses of Heart

Cover by Exceller Books

ISBN: 978-93-48892-59-1

First published in India in 2025 by Exceller Books,
An imprint of GE Group
Address: G1, Dream Apartment, Degree College Road, Belgharia,
Kolkata, 700056, India
www.excellerbooks.com

EXCELLER BOOKS®
A GLOBAL PRESS

Dedication

I would like to dedicate this book to my parents, my brother and friends who have always inspired me to write more and more for all.

Preface

The book, 'Euphoria: Glimpses of Heart' is a collection of sixty English poems with different kinds of themes and matters. This book will reveal not only the poet's inner thoughts but also the beautiful presentation of each poem, conveying immense happiness and creativity. Playing with words is an art that not everyone can master. The title of the book itself expresses its own joy through this bunch of poems. These poems encompass themes of friendship and love, praise of life and beauty, nature and its phenomena, supernatural entities, the philosophy of human life, death and sorrow, and, above all, the inspiration and joy of life. No particular meter is followed here.

Contents

Friendship

Friendship is a boon;
Softer than petals and lighter than feathers,
It makes us fly high above the sky.
True friends are like golden daffodils,
Dancing happily in waves.
Under this blue sky,
A shelter is a true friend—
Whom I call "dear,"
Wiping out my tears,
Filling my heart with joy.
You share, you care,
You're always calm to hear
What I bear—what I love to be for!
Isn't it lovely
How you teach me?
The best part is to live in,
Expecting nothing in return but love.
True friendship spans distance—
None is too vast.
It spans time—
Forever, it will last.
You're one of those special ones
With whom I shared joy and sorrow.
It is my great, indelible promise:
I will be with you today and tomorrow.

The Paragon: To My Inspirer

Dear, dear, dear! It is you
Who are always beside me and near,
Whenever I need to call you.
At last, I am free—
No more tied to mundane desires,
No more am I entangled in intricate emotions!
You compelled me to come out of fear—
Of losing myself in a chaos of pain.
Deep down, it's been nurtured—not in vain,
But to create a beautiful verse of love and loss.
Only by the impetus you shower upon me—
As plentiful as stars in the sky, glittering in glee.
Facing the day of cheers and sunshine,
Success is what we both acquire together—
Waving and shaking four hands, wishing happily.
By keeping your promise, I may propel far and far,
With rewards and reputation knocking at the door!
You, the dear one, are the absolute truth.
You are the giving force that holds me up high.
With glorifying gratitude, I try to worship you—
The one truly needed in life by none but a few like you.

Hope

"Hope" is the feeling
That carries you through.
Hope is the future,
Which is for me and you.
Hope is like a bird
That perches on our soul
And sings a song of belief
That won't be stopped at all.

"Hope" is the pillar
That stands alone in the gale.
Sweetest of all is heard
While you are dazed.
It neither leaves you alone
Nor pensive without words;
It is like a ripple of waves
That comes ashore and washes away.

"Hope" is a glee—
Strange, pleasant like the sea!
Yet never, in fatality,
Has it asked a shred of me.

The Flute

Chanting the name of Lord Krishna,
Songs of wisdom ring from the heart,
Letting you know the truth—
Life has a greater part for you to have.
Songs of love and experience we often play;
On the flute, it makes these sounds amazing.
As we hear, we feel a song that leads us to say:
A mind of vision can foresee what's next to happen!
Sit down and listen to the story of the eternal tune of bliss—
Of five thousand stories spoken about people and what they sought:
To plant a seed, to set us free from the world of desires.
Parents have both a song and a voice to sing,
To hear the echo of this flute in this very room—
Knowing who you are and the path you roam.
The journey of the soul is the cycle of life.
In the darkest journey, the days seem brighter.

Parents possess the sound of wisdom.
Before they play,
Just sit and listen to it—
Listen to the music they carry through the flute.

The Phoenix: A Journey of Resurrection

Like an eagle with shining red, golden, and purple plumes in Egypt,
Like the Sun God Ra depicted in mythology,
Springing forth from the pyre:
The Phoenix is a bird — the symbol of resurrection and rebirth.
Like a Phoenix, I will rise from the ashes
That enclosed me each time
You tried to make me feel burned within.
Suffocating in my tomb of agony, I borrow—
But I will learn to breathe life again:
Inhaling the fresh, new air and exhaling the battered you.
I will emerge to bid adieu to you forever,
Filling my lungs with clear and clean,
Shedding the past awhile,
As if you were never here beside me!
'Cause you threw me in the gutter like a stone,
Giving no value, you have neither regret nor pain.
To live, to laugh, to love once again,
I must be a Phoenix — to rise and fly.
Nothing can end this spirit ignited:
No wounds, injury, or demise.
Soaring again — I will. I can. I must!
For I am like the Phoenix eternal.

Alone

Gazing afar, too long,
Thinking profoundly:
Alone, lying on the bed,
Whispering, murmuring
A few words that I do.
I go, I laugh, I cry—
All alone. But nobody tries,
Tries to listen to what I'm saying.
Alone, I fight, I slip, I stand.
I wake up, recalling the memory;
I bear it all inside my heart.
Yes, all alone. I remember you,
While you totally forgot—
Forgot to tell: an aroma of love
I can often smell,
By myself, all alone.
But nobody,
Nobody can make it here all alone,
As I have devoured
Since you left me,
Made me lonely.
Sitting alone,
I set my soul free
With the pain of separation.

The Door

Yes! It is the Door—
It was the Door:
Between you and me—
You have now closed it,
Forever, or for moments fragile?
I really don't know.
The closer I come, the more I inhale a lot within,
Touch you, kiss you for a while—
Sounds of love so profound,
You know you've forgotten!
A lot I cried,
I cry the more you laugh.
The Door—you hit me on the mouth in front!
I crouched—yet still,
Nerves aching a while, you yell out.
The Door I've opened till now—
For you, only for you, Dear, my love—
To come near me, hold me tight,
Embrace me tightly, holding my hands,
With a promise of love—
To be mine forever and ever after a life,
Humming a verse of romance.
I warmly welcome your advent
Towards this Door to me, my Dear.

Delight

Warmed, soaked, and extracted for a while—so,
To be glad—damn, I care the way it goes.
To make it true—heart 'n' soul—free from all woes,
Morning dews on the grass, so fresh as they were.
Yesterday, today, and tomorrow will be the same:
Life is a game—once you fail, then you'll win.
A light in a dark hole, a light in an empty room,
Whispers in my ears a sound of boon.
Winter is coming soon.
Leaves are falling down,
Acorns patter while a sparrow shivers alone.
Down the hill, moaning, I sow a thought,
As if a robin or thrush sings
Of merry matters.
But the snow, once fallen
On the hueless grass,
Revives the zeal and beauty
By the winds as they pass.
Turns the climbing hedge
Into a gleaming ladder of frozen light.
And just—hark! In the cold, mesmerizing silence—
A shrill cry of delight!

Goodbye

Her love has faded,
Her faith is gone,
Hopes are down today,
She is moaning alone.
Two little words are these:
To bid you, dear—goodbye.
It means nothing, she knew.
Nothing can tremble you.
No emotions are left behind you.
The reason she has given—
Nought to know, you roam to and fro.
It's madness, but it's time to do so:
To stay strong, let the days of us pass by.
Let the music play, let the bee come;
A new man has come—
Let her feel you are gone!

Laptop, His Friend

When he wakes up from sleep,
When he loves to work again in the glee,
He opens his fingers to the keypad—
You know, it's his friend he calls *Laptop*.
From day to night, today to tomorrow,
He clicks the buttons and the wicked mouse,
Scrolling from Google to Yahoo.
Palms are always active, left and right.
What's next? He finds it right:
Working without it, working with it—just impossible to think!
He calls his dear pal, who is close to his bed, his *Laptop*.
Sweet little fellow, fits in his bag;
He can use it wherever he likes to go—
Travelling to games, secrets to fun,
His *Laptop* stores it all when the hard disks run.
The world in his hand, friends near to home,
Surfing the net broader than most ever roam.
You, the omnipresent *Laptop*—he needs you daily.
He believes it, too.

A Tint of Vermillion

A bright scarlet red or vivid orange!
Between two wide tracks, it means
A lot for a maiden who's going to tie the knot.
The red colour is itself the muse of love;
The range is strange between two wide tracks.
It's a holy night when they will find you
Among the jasmine and beautiful dew,
A wintry gust of wind and candlelight glimmering,
Waiting to drink a sip of nectar that boosts love
Between you two.
Only a tint of red or reddish-orange adorns your temples,
Blossoming with the touch of the rights of love you abide,
Singing a merry song from morning to night amidst the blue.
It's not a mere colour of red vermilion;
It's powerful, too,
As it saves you from those hungry demons
Who rush to devour—once, today, and tomorrow.

Stopping by the Empty Railway Station on a Wintry Evening

O, the darkness brought a quiet there.
The lamplight, shimmering on the railway station,
Was alone in the empty, crowdless space.
No heads to be found—only a dog's barking sound.
Ah! A chilly, wintry evening—
Hoarse, windy blast.
No stationary stalls were open,
Drizzling outside as I thrusted alone,
Probing for a human voice to call upon.
Locating none, I felt an awe within:
A cold and dark fear, shrilling down my spine,
Dumbed me through that dizzy eve,
Letting me feel when I shall pass—all yet so.
I crept down, remembering the holy God.
I smelt the earth, wetted from near and far.
The more I paced forward,
The nearer I could see a shadowy figure,
Waving one hand on such a foggy evening.
At last, I saw—and I was seen, whatever else.
The drizzle continued, with a cool breeze to and fro.
The man was semi-old, a kind auto driver,
Wearing a ragged shawl and a battered muffler.
He offered me a cup of tea and drove me along.

The Last Meeting Together

We were sitting together on the cemented chairs in a field.
Our hands were entangled in a mood of joy.
You thought of moving from your distant home—
Everything I can bear except separation.
You were lost in pensive thoughts,
While I whispered in your ear something to say:
That I can't live without you.
Suddenly, you dragged me close,
Maddened me by showering kisses!
It seemed to me the bitterest one, as if
It were the last touch you had given.
You detached your lips and fumbled to convey,
In a very low voice, "When I'm no longer beside you,
Remember my endless kisses, though."
My world seemed volatile.
My entire body became numb and cold—
To think: a moment of emptiness
That never was, after we met each other.

One Night in a Brothel

Peeping through an old window,
We were virile eighteens once upon a time.
We saw a mattress layered on the floor,
Wild jasmine decorated the rooms,
Shiny curtains quivered in a cool breeze.
We were mesmerized to watch her—
Lips smeared red, dark, and swollen,
Eyes shining black and bordered profoundly.
Her hair was loosely held by a pointed pin,
Cheeks coloured reddish-pink, and a glossy chin.
A red dot of vermillion perhaps darkened her forehead.
Hips swayed in emphasized measure,
Her breasts were full, riding on bashful waves.
Chuckling, giggling—as fast as we could see—
Her arms were embraced by many men's hands.
Shoes were scattered hither and thither on the stairs,
Hustle and bustle on the narrow lane as virile eighteens peered.
The fascinating smell of wild perfume maddened us.
We saw those men in black sprawling out without shame.
They snatched away clothes one by one from the women...
From beginning to end, it was an erotic, oppressive game.
We were shocked—speechless to feel a filthy one—
No feelings, no emotions left behind;
Two machinery bodies united to be the sole one.

Black Magic

Amidst the deep, dark woods, in the magic of night,
Two lovers' fire of love ignites!
It is a secret within a heart—
How they connect, though far apart.
She gazes up with her weary smile,
The little brook flowing down beside...
In his grotto, the maiden sits alone, aside.
A strong black magic spell,
Swirling between them,
Driving her insane,
Making him crazy.
Her fathomless ebony eyes,
Evening sunset beside,
Beneath the banyan tree—
The closer the two of them,
The more they are to be free.
Heart to heart, breathing alike so fast:
Lips locked, heavenly feelings abashed.
Secret passages of lovers' escape,
Familiarity in its black cape.
Their consummate passion is lurking in fashion—
Darkness, the colours profound as unknown;
Sibylline eyes call upon the mystery at home.

The Leader

A leader is You, a leader is wise,
A leader is someone we do not despise.
It's not about power, wealth, or fame—
True leadership is not a game.
A leader is You, a leader is kind,
A leader always leads from behind.
A leader stands and stays till day's end,
And aches for the way we think, as we may break.
A leader is You, a leader is nice,
A leader is someone who gives good advice.
A leader serves the poor, mostly those in need—
They are authentically soulful indeed.
An honour born of strength within,
A leader never escapes—
But holds a courage that stands alone,
And rarely gives in.
Their virtue is generous, humble, and just.
They do right for all, against the unjust.
A leader is selfless; a leader can be You.
Leadership is not about the power to reign,
But a noble service to mankind we gain.
A leader is You, a leader is Me—
A leader is someone anyone can be.

Illusion

Real or false, it is truly enigmatic to know;
Our virtual world is wrapped in reality,
Forming a mist of intricate maze—
What to do, what not to,
Null and void in gaze.
Painting the grass with clouds of water,
Ambushing the sleeping bugs
With the dropless rain.
O hear! This life is nothing but a mere illusion.
Let me roam like an eagle, freely;
Let me soar higher than the blue sky—really.
Give me the sunshine to soak my wet vision,
Warmed thoroughly by the blazing sun.
Scorching heat, sandy, windful blust—
An elusive spark that ignites my thirst.
What a view! What a life!
It is a merry-go-round;
We fight like Tom and Jerry.
Dreaming high above the sky,
Stars guide me through a glowing hue.
I rig for a journey, search for a man
To hold my arms in the depths of the ocean,
Charging the voyage through this illusion.

An Architect of Dreams: To the Headmaster

Look at the gait,
Look at the attire
HE gets.
Look at his hands,
Raised high for all — pupils —
In the morning light.
With the shrill sound of the bell,
His voice wafts through the corridor.
Blooming pupils hear and face,
With shuttered ears, divining his voice.
The dim pupils see only what is said.
Foundation laid with care and skill —
Upon his wisdom, we build our will.
Dreams constructed, brick by brick,
By a headmaster's touch — astute and quick.
We believe his words, fathom his morals;
We follow his footprints more and more, in glee.
HE is the pillar, an impetus for all,
Ethically guiding us through firm principles.
How a headmaster trains on the heel —
A dagger strikes, the paper cuts —
See his exalted force before those,
By making the impossible possible, too.
And the student — boy or girl — submissively lies
At his feet, with due respect and a new view.
Outside the school, HE is grossly heard;
Nothing against him is charged.
HE is the *Supremo*,
HE is like a leader.
The path to success HE has drawn —
From now and then.
We are so grateful for each pillar HE placed,
For every challenge HE gracefully faced.
Architect of every dream — to him, all of us raise
A salute for the bright future HE will embrace.

Every Woman

It is for every woman,
Who is the pillar of the house.
She is beautiful,
She is the giving force
Amidst the blue.
She is the womb,
She is the power.
It is for every woman
Who is a mother,
Who spends sleepless nights
For hours and hours;
Staying awake, she lies on the bed.
It is for every woman
Who is scared of being hurt again,
Who has been left behind, heartbroken;
Who needs to be given
Something to believe in.
She is an enchanting *femina*,
With intuitive eyes.
She can smell from so far
In ways no one can imagine.
She knows how to react, but
Often remains silent.
She needs to be nurtured within.
She longs to feel desirable,
Now and then.
It is for every woman
Who speaks up freely,
Who wants to be loved again,
Who cares deeply,
And accepts all for who they are.
For every woman, a man—
Though that's not always the case.
A bachelor or a spinster,

You will find them in every place.
A man for every woman:
It is not always true.
A woman is born free;
She can choose her life,
Just as a man can do.
Some never have a partner,
And without a partner, they die.
And for everyone, there is someone—
Though in some cases, it is a lie.

The Haunted House

See the gloomy walls, with weedy creepers grow;
See the dim, broken lamp-light flickering slow.
Smell the wild scent of deep woods behind;
Touch the green moss around the terrace you find.
Oh, very, very dreary is the room!
Where bond, domestic love, no longer nestles,
But, smitten by the common stroke of doom,
The corpse lies on the trestles so!
Feel it—feel the house of woe, hearse, and sable pall:
The narrow home of a departed mortal
Ne'er looked so gloomy as that ghostly hall,
With its deserted portal.
Recall the past memory, with the sweetest fragrance tripling,
As lavender and daffodils dance, dwelling under the same canopy.
See the undisturbed patch of cobweb as a prehensile cell
Of moth or maggot, or spider's tissues do.
Footsteps are obstructed on the stairs, as they're broken too.
A sense of mystery, the spirit daunted—
A fear of an abandoned house robbed calmness,
And said, as plain as a whisper in the ear,
That the house is haunted.

An Old Banyan Tree

O, massive Old Banyan Tree,
Standing alone near the pond,
To be born as free.
Your trunks are bigger than others;
Your roots are stronger, as we know.
Many hundred your aerial roots—
You give shade to the tired travellers,
Giving nests to the tiny birds, too.
When the wind blows strong so,
Your branches are fearless, swaying as though.
Providing shelter and water to anyone you don't know,
You are the great, kind Old Banyan Tree to whom we love to bow.
The pond near you is the bathing place of little pigeons and sparrows.
Our eyes are overwhelmed to see the lotus floating there in a row.
As a tribute to you, noble, great Banyan Tree—
You are the oldest one, the living thing we see.
It's a joy; it's a pure feeling,
To watch your arms swinging like a bee.

I Am a Slum Boy

Hopeless, homeless,
Like a vagabond,
Roaming to and fro.
No flowery bed is where I grow,
No tree to give a shadow,
No tiny branches to swing,
And to play where I go.
I used to play with gutter stones,
All alone, all alone.
On brown summer days, I wake up,
I sit and play with tiny, lean-faced playmates.
As evening sets in,
I steadily walk on damp, narrow lanes,
With dim lamp lights on each side.
Shades of light and dark are my tale of life.
I beg, I often steal unwillingly;
For food and rest, I'd creep up the stairs,
Or, empty-bellied, lie and sleep,
With a silence of profound weep.
No parents to care often,
No care to be shown.
I am thirsty for the hands of love,
I am a Slum Boy.
O wondrous life! My wordless woe,
I worry about my present time,
For living a good life.
What evil, filthy poverty
Devours me in my childhood!
I can't smile like them,
I can't sing a happy song.
In spite of this merciless fate,
I try to be calm, although
To know a bare truth—
Of eternal peace must flow.

Secretly blossomed, a dirty boy I am;
People hate me often.
I groan up out of emotion.
I search for an eye,
Search for a hand,
To hold me tight, raise me up,
To the sky, to the sky.
My voice is endless,
My roar is rare.
O mystery of life,
I am not special yet—
But ignored, not at all, although, although.
Give me wings, give me the path,
Give me life, give me love.
I am like you, although a Slum Boy.

The Burning Riot in Bangladesh

Looking around the country,
The riot scene is harsh.
Hindu men and women are homeless, abandoned,
Weeping helplessly, scattered on the ground.
Threats from Muslims, with bitter hatred toward them—
Communal agony fills my heart with pain.
Violence, blood—everywhere is seen.
We want this riot to end,
But no ears are eager to pay attention.
Noises of riot, with fierceness,
Killing lives, killing peace—
The images are truly hopeless.
Where men are busy with cruelty,
In the place of death, or the fireplace,
I pray to God for peace and calmness.

The Witch

One chilly night,
The wild wind blows,
The leaves rustle and move.
In the dark night, the full moon glows.
A dog barks in the distance,
A cat yawls from far,
Mice are creeping to and fro,
Spiders' cobwebs are there.
Lights go on at every house—
It's almost the witching hour.
They will appear soon,
As all manner of ghosts,
Witches, and goblins do.
We hear the uncanny sounds there;
It's dreary, too.
Suddenly, the doorbell rings.
Suddenly, the windowpane jerks.
Do I open? Do I dare to answer?
What's coming next for me if I do so, too?
Blinking of the lights,
Darkness around the room—
I found smoke swirling upright,
Shaping a figure out.
What to do, what not to do?
Do I ask? Do I dare?
My eyes are wide open,
Reframing the sight:
TRICK Or TREAT, It's a Halloween Night.

The Lost Love

In the summer's lap once,
The blooming love was engrossed,
With aromatic blue petals
We once cherished to see.
There's one whom you belonged to—
Your heart beat every second for me;
You uttered my name in glee, lovingly.
Once, you felt—
You knelt before me,
With a bunch of pink roses,
Embraced me happily.
There was a time when
We rode together,
As joyful as we knew;
Stars guided us, though.
You, my love, once shared emotions that,
With passion and care, I bore in my heart.
Till then and today, I have felt the same.
I have missed you each time.
Every day, I set myself to you,
As a free soul to breathe in.
Once, you really cared,
Kissed me so long.
I really missed its warmth—
You really don't know.
Your ego, your harshness ended it all,
And broke me, too.
Your betrayal stabbed me back.
Nothing is as dreadful as it is to think.
I feel pain, for you wronged me.

An Evening at Trincas

What a decorum!
How yellow and blue lights hang below,
Plastic creepers, petals of white orchids in a row.
What merry laughter around Park Street!
Oh yeah! It's fine—Christmas Eve—you look at it.
People, hither and thither, are gathering slowly;
In the light and dark, charms are aroused glowingly.
Men and women, clothed in fashionable hues, gossip a lot,
Where ten fingers and the glass mingle with a new applause.
Either to hide one's pain or to celebrate one's joy,
A glass of wine or whiskey can be better with you.
Remembrance of Quinto Cinizio Trinca, Joseph, Flury, and so on—
The gala music of it just sways the dizzy mind full-on.
Oh! The live concert—wavy lyrical magic—
Maddens them all, intoxicates, and blurs the vision,
More than they absorb and sip for too long.
Kissing the lips or kissing the wine glass,
Lovers have just embarked on Dreamland blust.

Perfume

I dream so far and far,
I smell so refreshing.
My senses are heightened, though,
As the aroma fills the air.
Swiftly awakening memories
I would long forget were there,
As if to cuddle me too long,
To kiss me warmly.
What gift for two passionate lovers can I find?
Neither the books nor the flowers suffice for me.
When I feel the glam fragrance—
Odorous cedar tree or rose petals,
Tufts of pine bud, wetted woods, oozy in the wind—
Give me young shoots of aromatic rind,
Of samphire, redolent of sea and sand.
For all such fragrances, I deem them to be
Fit with my sharp desires to be combined.
Mind is poetic to draw a room
Of scents engrossed with jasmine and pink lilies—
Dried rose leaves, sticks of tuberose, and sandalwood mingled up,
Arousing a superb aroma and filling the room.
From curtain to window pane, its vibes are just getting on.
I am thinking of him for long, in a never-ending way.
I am searching for a path, a sign of smell!
It is an incredible perfume that never leaves me away.

The Mad Woman

Mad, mad, mad...
See the mad woman,
With promiscuous, curly hair,
Dusty body, ragged clothes, lying in the dirt.
The road was full, and was laughing at her;
Some cruels were spitting on her,
And twitching her hands for fun.
Poor, helpless to find none,
She screamed out in vain.
Her broken bowl dropped down,
Her torn satchel was lost in the crowd.
She, the wretched woman, wept more.

Casanova

A woman's dream is high —
Tall, fair, handsome, flattering mouth,
Telling all the time a lie.
He has his charming eyes,
Captivating smile, provoking posture,
As walking beside and by.
Riding in his car,
Entangled in his arms,
Every woman wants to be his queen.
But he is a flaw, a damn flirt,
Never makes a promise to keep in.
All kinds of things he will do,
He will bow with a red rose...
But in reality, it is a real trap,
When the game of love ends up.
Cheating is his motto,
Breaking up his excuse;
He loves to fall in love—
Once, twice, and so on.

Oracion

Once upon a time, I was swaying, dream-divine;
I wished to be thine forever and ever so...
I wished I had a cradle to swing—
With you... mine alone, so high!
Desiring a moonlit night,
Walking, feet together, twining afar.
I wish, I wish to be thine...
With arms embracing me, cuddling nearer.
I dream of receiving the light,
A call or whisper triggering me...
Gaze fixed on an igniting sconce;
Waiting there to dine together.
I feel free to rush,
Feel free to smooch once...
To say I love you.

Once upon a time, I was dreaming at night.
I wished to ring you,
Wished to be with you...
Praying heart and soul to be united together.

The Devil

A little devil stays inside my head —
I have not seen him yet.
I am sure that he is red.
Luminous mind, bright devil,
Of absolute clusterings, of upright noon —
Here I am at last alone, without loneliness,
Far from the city's delirium.
Those times when I feel happy,
He will stoke a fire for me.
My good moon is replaced then
By full-on anxiety.
The mind and love live naked in this house,
As the pure line describes the dove's curve,
As the fire honours and nourishes peace,
So you and I made this heavenly promise.
Furious dreams, a river of bitter certainty,
Decisions scattered to and fro abruptly.
In my sleeping time, he rose up high,
Whispering subconsciously in continuity.
It is hard to escape him;
It is hard to believe in...
He is too clear to my ears.
I hate this little demon...
Wanna drive away so far...
Leaving him, I wish to set myself free,
To kiss the sky as a bird to fly...
Next to another haven, I remain,
From diseased devil free.

The Glory

The day fills with an amorous blue sky;
Pensive eyes can see the cuckoos sing and fly.
The rattling window calls, the sun vims inside,
The coconut tree is dancing in glee.
The glory of beauty I see in the rising sun—
Burning yellow and orange-tinged glow.
White clouds range high...
The heat I felt in my heart exhaled in a sigh.
The sky, meadow, and forest call me to widen below—
Besides the lovely motion of the river flowing in a natural hue.
In beauty's presence, wisdom or strength can start,
A new day filled with hope and happiness to show
That in hope I find to provide whatever I seek.
Or, asking, must I be content with discontent,
As the larks and swallows fly without wings?
And shall I query the day's end once more:
What is the beauty? What is the glory to be called?
What do I feel to mean it?
By happiness, shall I pass them all like a drop of dew...?
Or shall I let go?
I promptly whisper a sound of grand glory—
Knowing not the upcoming call of future,
Knowing not the present bell of joy.
I just see and clap for the season's happiness,
Amidst the nature and blue.
I rush to the flying kite at my playmate's one call,
That I am happy oft and oft before I play,
Forgetting the weary past, how I am fast pent,
How bitterly swift!
With nothing left to keep beside,
Isn't it time so?
I fairly can't bear all the fleeting moments as I go.

Amnesia

If I ever forget you, lose my mind,
Will you read this to me?
It could perhaps help me
Trigger back my memory.
Tell me about all the candlelight dinners, sitting for two,
And all those intimate things I have done to you.
Speak of the sun burning bright for us,
Speak of the dewdrops that fell on the grass last night.
Speak of the sound of the train whistling from afar to our ears,
The weekend rain, talk about the loss, happiness, and pain, embracing us.

Paint a picture of the dress you loved to wear,
Tell me how I liked to play with your curly hair.
Draw the landscape where we beautifully spent time together—
Tell me about the trees on which I used to swing thither.
Tell me about the birds chirping and perching around the ceiling of her nest.
Describe to me the variety of those books I loved to read.
And tell me about the old cat you used to feed.
Tell me about the small ponds, café shops, and our favourite flowers;
What about the hot summer when we made love for hours?
Please talk about the night when the tears I shed hit your chest,
And I whispered out, "You're simply the best."

If I ever forget you, lose my mind to the way,
Take me back to yesterday, give me a kiss,
And let me eagerly stay.

If my mind never strikes me to remember you,
Tell me about you, from beginning to end, all the way—
I am certain I will recall to love you all over again, I say.

The Hidden Treasure

Our hearts are burning
Over the loss of a treasure.
Pain in our hearts,
Sorrows in our minds,
Tears in our eyes,
Grief in our veins,
Rippling with confusion in the chain.

I found a shiny gold penny—
Nineteen thirty-one—my grandma was born.
My memories with her are in this one cent,
And all that I have—the penny—is priceless.
I recalled her face and touched her feet in my vision.
Grandma was telling a tale of a fairy with passion.
I felt her wrinkled skin over her shades of memories...
I knelt before her to watch the pearl-like eyes she carried.
Everything—useless compared to my special treasure
I found in her—became moan when she passed away.
At the thought of that, tears slid down my cheek,
Like the rain walking beside me, and grandma picking it.
How I yell alone, how I miss...
I wish to bring the penny back into my life.
I remember her gentle talk,
A soft touch on me.
I miss her day and night,
Whenever I see the photograph together.
Grandma, my hidden treasure, is now away from me,
To the far heaven I can't go,
Can't touch her so.
She was the gem,
She was the pearl—
Away from the earthly haven,
Hidden from this world.
But visible in my mind,
Every moment in grief, I sigh;
Treasure of a loving heart—
Like a diamond beneath the earth,
Hidden in my heart.

Ecstasy

My love,
Carry me in your arms to the Paradise.
There, forever, let me stay by your side.
In love, I dream of the high—
Spreading my wings to fly...
To kiss the blue heaven,
To touch the spell of clouds.
I can feel the joy, enlightened with you.
A sweet zephyr wind blows around us.
Let us fly more to this zenith of love,
As we sit and walk together for long—
A journey to the far, I play a sweet song.
I shall be yours; you will be mine!
The oath is crystal clear;
It is so strong
That my love for you is an endless joy,
With the pace of time.
As we taste Heaven in true love's kiss,
You give me your heart; I give you mine!
The heart is full of blooming petals.
You cannot deny—
I love, and I will be loving you.
My promise is firm.
In love, I will be with you;
The ecstasy of my love will be going on.

Gem in the Eyes

You make me laugh with teary eyes,
You make me cranky sometimes,
But you make me happy most of the time.
Your soft skin—so lovely to touch—
I believe in you so much.
You are the apple of my eyes;
I feel warmed to get your advice.
The gem you are—so I mean,
The gem with you I deem.
For what your smile makes me crazy,
I was having insomnia, although I was drowsy.
My precious gem, I am overwhelmed;
I feel like thanking the universe
For the one who cheered me up when I was scorned.
You amazed me well to win my heart.
Like a gentle breeze, you are always smart.
I am lucky to have you in my life—
A blessing for which I am thankful to life.

The Sleeping Cat

Tiny little eyes, alien yellow,
Snow-like white fur and a black tone:
That is my baby cat, sitting on a place hollow.
Its meowing and its cries
Let me feel it—a noisy fellow.
My baby cat is a cute one,
Sprawling here and there alone.
It walks on all four limbs,
It roams in daytimes.
While it sleeps like a kid of a man,
Without a care in the world,
Without a fear in its life,
It dreams of food to eat.
The cat sits asleep when I call it.
It is a tensionless fellow,
Brightened with a glossy glow.
I feel so happy to see it sleepy.

My Motherland

What glory around You!
What fragrance I smell for You!
You are the Holy Motherland,
A heritage to our soul,
Never to be apart from us alone.
The vast sky, the ocean blue, and the forest deep grown,
The widened green field calls me to be free.
I see a solitary reaper singing a scythe song,
On the narrow way to the valley.
The cuckoo, the sparrow, together, and the peacock's song,
Glim with the temple chants.
The Ganges and the Yamuna reside,
The grand Himalayas are mystic so.
I recall the moment of Independence Day,
Holding the tri-coloured flag in pride,
Emancipated with the national anthem.
I recall the past—Jawan's chivalry.
O, holy land, You are a history,
Unity in diversity—you bear a mystery.
With joyous celebration of festivals,
I ruminate about the sun and the moon,
Flood and struggle,
The happy song of human sorrow.
The sagacity and the gravity we call for,
The great Himalaya—mystic so.
Down the ages, the land is a dream for us.
The divine grace and the mythology we read,
Following the path of spirituality.
With its manifold, India is rich in its actuality.
With a deep spirit and a patriotic heart,
Everyone loves to bow to You as Your loving son.

I Miss You

O fire of my heart,
The flower of my soul,
You are a very special one
I want to call.
In your absence, my days and nights
Are a burden to me—a heavy plight.
Without you, days are endless,
Without you, nights are joyless.
Everything seems so empty,
I feel so lonely.
You are the spark of my smile.
You are the source of my force.
Moments with you are frozen in time.
I miss you, darling; you're like my enzyme.
Your face appears whenever I turn.
Painful it is—the love they've made me yearn.
Without you, I feel life's demise—
You are mine and my dearest prize.
You yell out so high,
You use foul words on me.
You deny your love—so igniting—for me.
You can't see the pain;
I try to let go, although in vain.
My strength is weakening,
Cold days seem endless;
Lonely, sorrowful nights often begin.
I beg of you to come back soon,
Hold me tight, embrace me once,
Feel me with emotions.
I'm left with a broken heart;
Nothing in the world can tear us apart.
Only you can—willingly so;
You've done.
I'll count the moments till we reunite,
Sending all my love through the day and night.

First Light

A cycle of seasons is going on—
Crimson sun sets in.
An evening's call to me,
From afar, I can hear:
The busy beetle murmuring,
As the cricket is whispering.
Around, a chilly darkness possesses—
I can hear an owl's screech and all.
O, the sun will rise up soon,
On the next day, with its boon,
To give us warmth and the first light.

In light and dark, life's journey is beginning—
The first twig of a plant,
The first bee perched on the flower.
As we see the most beautiful thing of joy,
It's forever and ever...
The wondrous nature is filtering us
From dirt and dust.

Bliss

Another day comes,
Another hope runs; mystically, so it does.
I love to cling to the bough of dreams—
Shivering within my bosom, although!
Can you hark the call of the sky?
Do you know why the road diverged there?
Everything resides in nature; mystically, so it does.
The first chirp of a sparrow,
The first chick of the hen—
See them with blissful joy in the rain.
O hear the spring's joyous call!
The beauty, hence, never fades away.
To far and far, I glance in glee
To feel its charm.
The baby on her mother's lap,
Babbling with a toy,
Seems to me a blissful joy.
God's grace is unfathomable—
How omnipresent He is!
In sorrow, His grace feels
So divine, and like an incomparable joy.

The Sea-Voyage

Sailing across the vast sea,
In the grey mist goes a sailing ship,
Filled with promising dreams,
And blindly steering an unknown course,
Charted by uncertain schemes.
Seated all on deck, we floated
Down the Rhine's majestic dreams;
On its borders, summer-laden,
Slept the peaceful evening gleam.
Lutes were ringing, and youths were singing,
Swelling my heart with feelings strange;
Bluer grew the heaven above us,
Wider grew the spirit's range.
I wonder how the hulk of Odysseus,
On the seamless ocean, might have felt—
His tired sailors,
Drinking salt and yellow sunlight,
And peering over a bowsprit of hope
To behold some friendly haven.
These mariners,
Sailing on Homer's wine-dark sea—
The sight of every grain of sand,
As exciting as an aphrodisiac.

The Poet and His Muse

What a relation it is
Between the poet and his muse!
I found him never married to his muse.
She is the impetus or stimulus, he calls—
The goddess of each poem he composes.
His love for her is endless; something that she denies.
Love's road ends in marriage.
When he told her this,
With a gentle kiss on her forehead,
She got a shock.
Remembering her name and face,
The poet invokes words—
Words alluring him with a fever of passion.
The days passed in pensive thoughts;
Each day, for them, a new plight.
Each day, he recalls her name for a fight.
Time is fleeting, and so is the spell
Upon the couples I get.

Love's road ends in marriage.
They feel so inseparable,
Tying the knot in heaven.

The Prophecy

A little while, my longing shall gather stones from the riverside...
A little while, *ozora* of mind is craving for a twilight...
Azure sky, full of clouds gleaming low—
The darkness makes me free.
Suddenly, I ruminate on the youth
I spent with you;
It was so lovely and delightful.
You have sung to me in aloneness,
I have built a tower of prophecy...
To meet you another day in a dream—
It will come true.
If, in the memory lane, we should meet again,
Wake up fast to live to the fullest, regressing pain.
If our hands are together, allured,
We will make a tower of love, for sure.

The Veil

Who is behind the veil?
Who looks through it?
Front, to and fro?
Who sees what others
Only think they feel?
Who gives hope
And hands out fate?
Who has the keys
To freedom's gate?
Who loves to walk through
The passage of heart?
Who has the power
To win over?
Who keeps the secrets
From you and me?
Who has those hands
To lift us up?
The mind has its layers
To separate every thought.
Who can pass on—
Never be told, untold?
We look through the window
To the horizon, above and below.
We must go on
To cross the wall of life—
Who knows what's coming next?
To hold us, to be adorned,
Who creates the veil?
Who lurks behind the veil,
Behind the veil alone?

Nostalgia

When I am alone,
I can see so far—the old banyan tree,
Swinging happily its branches below the sky.
I can smell the fragrance of rose petals
From the little garden my mom has made.
I can hear a group of tiny sparrows and nightingales,
Chirping their words and singing melodiously.
I can feel the sky and its moving clouds,
The tiny little marigolds, dancing in glee.
I can recall my childhood playmates—
My school days are gone.
I can visualize the noise in the classroom,
And the teachers teaching us all.
When I am cradling alone,
Pensive dictions triggering me soon,
I am compelled to think of the old days of happiness, which were adorned.
I can see the kitchen and my mom cooking so fast.
The smell of delicious soup tempts me a lot.
The delicacy of each memory enhances my joy—
I feel so solicitous about what invokes my past.
I thrillingly drill through those, one by one.
With the hammer of each word
I write,
I ruminate about the days gone by—happily and free.
To the lake swims the swan, green;
The doves nest beautifully on the mango tree.
I can browse my drawing book of old landscapes
That I had drawn with the vibrant colours of love and joy.
I feel the same. I am here, and the colours are not gone.
I call myself to the time—fleeting, near and far.
I restore the enthusiasm I had left in the far past;
It can be revived and revised with a new passion.
When the sun sets in,

And I am alone in the room—
I can smell the near future calling me,
Through the glass window,
To be modest and justified in action,
New hopes of growth to follow.
I jerk my mind, twirling for a while;
I can talk to myself with vision's glow—
To do the best further, once upon a time.
Time passes on, around us and below.

Songs of Innocence

Every delight comes from a joy and light.
Every morn and every night,
Some to misery are born to fight;
Every morn and every night,
Some are born to sweet delight.
Some call to sweet memory
Of the frost of the past night.
With joy gleaming high,
Some sorrows are born to sigh.
We are led to believe a lie
Of life and death, showing a goodbye.
When we see not through the eye,
When we squat back on the lane,
A moonlit night is born to perish the dark night.
When the souls sleep in beams of light,
God appears there to give light—
To those poor souls who dwell in darkness,
To those who feel life as night,
So deep and having no light.
But so does the human form display
To those who dwell in the realms of day.
Appetite of life calls the poet
To create a world of surreal beauty.
Pleasure and success fill life
With a bounty.
Calm, pure, and sacred to see—
To feel the aura of blissful joy,
The poet invokes the Muse's resonance.
Everyone feels the utmost splendour,
Imbibed with such mesmerizing *Songs of Innocence.*

An Evening's Call

Cooling breeze with scents so sweet,
Under a muffled gray mist,
The Moon rises like a morning sun,
Giving the light of care and love a fist.
Shades of evening everywhere,
Gone the heat with my cares,
Melted—two hearts to be free.
The day has finally met defeat,
Shades of the evening at my feet.
O, the glowing moon on the starry sky,
The calmness whispers aloud;
One can glean a secret call—
No escape door to fly.
As the twilight wraps around,
Time to observe and not to talk;
As the evening invades the cooling ground,
Shades of evening in my hometown.
An evening covers the whole,
I can watch the moon's black hole.
As the beetles and crickets call,
I can hear it clearly—so near and far.
The mystery of an evening's charm
Never denies telling
That one can compose an evening tale.

Mystery of an Island

At a far distance away,
In the midst of a vast ocean,
Lies a mysterious island.
As the folk stories tell,
The island appears to be a wonder.
Dazzling with colourful lights,
After a day of heavy rain,
A magic, grand rainbow appears,
Like a crown of glittering lights.

Then, a graceful young lady,
Wearing a white gown,
Stands on the top of the hill alone,
Waving with her beautiful hands,
Holding a magical stick.
What's next to happen—
It is really a joy of wonder.
A rainbow colour appears,
The colour of the red.
The trees turn red,
Then, the sky ahead.
The green grass, the moon,
The valley, the river—
All become red in hue.
The moon smiles and turns red, too.
The heavy rains pour again,
The halo of rainbow colour,
So beautiful, stark, and bright.

The young lady comes again,
Waving her magic wand so new,
Wearing an orange gown;
She puts the colour everywhere.
Everything turns orange with a gale.

The rainbow now appears with
Seven colours, pal,
And fills the island with a magical ball.

This is a mystery of this island.
The tale of its glory,
Generation after generation will carry.
Is it real, or totally fairy?

An Everlasting Joy

Once,
On a sunny morning,
Uttered a little cry.
Pierced the little shell,
With her tiny little egg tooth,
To smell the soil,
To hear the chirps,
To learn to fly.

One day,
Mother gave her soft feathers.
Now,
She flies to touch the sky,
The vast blue sky,
With vibrant hues of desires—
Weaves the nest,
To give away
The feathers of her mother;
Caresses the newborn,
To kiss the infinite.

Love and Destiny

My love,
As pure as a white blossom for you.
Glowing the sun, shining the moon,
Tell you a love tale, of course.
I have lost the man I loved;
I have lost my peace...
My love has burnt me into ashes onwards;
I recalled him now, recalled him then;
I know he won't come back again.
Roses bloom in spring to make love attune,
My rose petals dried soon.
It's not called God's boon.
My love,
It has been destined to be apart,
Apart too far.
I know my walk will be slow without you,
But it has been destined to walk slow.
Tomorrow, I can say I will win,
Definitely, to grab me within.
I shall pass, too—
I, as proposed to do.

The Song of Fraternity

The child is born,
The child will speak to earn.
The child, one day, asks everyone:
Do you want
Worldwide happiness?
Sing the song of fraternity.
Sing the song to be united,
To be together in happiness and sorrow,
Tomorrow and tomorrow...
We can see the picture of this bond.
We call it a strength to obey.
The child is naked but true,
The child is not far away.
It is the mirror, the consciousness
Through which we can pass our lives
To sing the song of unity.
Do you want
Prosperity to touch the sky?
Peace to be established in the world
We live and go...?
Then, you must sing the song of fraternity.
Although we utter a word of friendship,
The child says to make it true.

Mirage

Amidst the melancholy songs,
Life is full of pangs.
It is truly changed —
As if into a small circle,
I feel like I'm caged.
The rose blossoms, although;
We smile, although;
Depression drove me
To daily toil!
Out of solitude,
The mind begins to boil.
Life is never fresh;
How can I alone relish to refresh?
Impossibilities grow;
The mind flees to and fro!
Life is worse than hell;
Untold woes — to whom shall I tell?
Life is an illusion;
True love you hardly find.
Learnt and learnt —
Love is a mirage of the mind!

Solitude

Mild the mist was upon the hill,
I closed my eyes to see its zeal.
The rainbow, as it passed
Through the clouds, it felt;
I felt the golden daffodils
Dancing beside the mounds.
I felt a serenity with such calmness;
Around me, the cool breeze
Enthralled like a bee.
I missed them all I visualized;
I knew there was none beside me.
O, these little dewdrops on green grasses,
I meant to soothe my eyes' tears;
I felt my nature's cry deep down,
Neither in glee nor in gloom.

The Last Sea Voyage

Little drops of water make a vast sea.
One higher desire once came from my home, and I fled.
With my luggage tightly taken,
To enjoy the last sea voyage, awaken.

My ship boarded from my port.
I felt there were dangers a lot.
Yet I ventured on my adventure,
To make a history for people to remember.

Over my head was the never-ending sky;
I knew, like a bird, I wanted to fly.
Then came a stormy night—
Afraid, we were about to fight.

Over the sea, a gusty wind blew;
What would be coming next, we never knew!
The darkness around us snatched the light.
One by one, inside the ship, we all lost our sight.

I thought the chapter of my life was about to end,
And someone to pick me up had been sent.
I knew that I had to go a long way in my life—
Holding my breath fearfully was to thrive.

The waves of the sea rose so high;
The gusty storm swirled and passed by.
My fellow rovers sighed aloud,
My eyes fixed on all to prolong the crowd.

It was a dreadful evening that we had ever faced;
Perhaps it was an unusual event, we guessed.
Life and death were so near,
Holding each other's hands tightly to cheer.

We were saved, we were alive;
The sea storm was stopped in our lives.

Silence

There is a two-folded silence—
The Sun and the Sea,
The Body and the Soul—
Play a lonely role.
Newly with grace overgrown,
Passion-stricken solemnity.
Dark with these human memories,
The tearful lore.
Rendering peacefully,
The name I utter is no more.
The very You is the corporate silence,
Dreadful, in short.
No evil game is there.
Wordless, I admire.
Fate comes to us suddenly,
Bright and lovely to see.
Power to revive meadow—
Bring me forth out of the shadow.

Reminiscence

Behold! The moon tells the story of your past.
The light comes forth to smell my whim's frost.
The scent of jasmine, sweet and pure,
A swing set swaying, time to endure.
Through the dusty corners of my mind,
A whisper of laughter, once so kind.
I go back to the dale with a stroke of gale;
A memory comes to me in glee.
The sweet pinch of love and its gift,
Throwing me back once in a swift.
The worn-out teddy, a faithful friend,
A storybook's tale that knows no end.
A shimmering glow in the twilight rush,
A tender touch and my lover's blush.
Now, like a river, time flows on,
Yet, in my heart, the past lives on.
A drapery of such moments, woven tight,
I follow these golden echoes in fading light.

Humanity

One unknown call reminds me of you,
Reminds me of the boughs of love,
Spreading for you...
The love I hold with me, for joy
And mercy, to sing a song of fraternity.
Being so human in flesh and blood,
I write the lyrics of bond and affinity
Between me and the universe.
The world before me sighs and laughs,
To hug me as a whole part of this path.
I will certainly spread—
I will spread the love of equality
To all I see; I care too much.
I will show them the way to be close,
For each other to be engrossed,
To feel free to be together,
With heart and soul to be near,
To give light in sorrow so far.

One Life

Think before you act;
Life is one to preserve.
Think before you act;
Life is none without work.
Happiness and fulfilment
Struggle to converge.
As the mind frames in changing colour,
It clings to the past in fear.
Think before you say;
Words can, too, hurt.
Live life to the fullest;
Live life and show.
Life leaps with death and rebirth—
Of thoughts and intentions,
Of memories and experiences,
Flashing inward for an unseen fortitude.

Let Me Have the Patience

Let me have the patience to see.
Let me have the courage to flee.
Let my patience call me to fly;
I want to wait and cry.

Let the light of love be enkindled!
Let the joy become my strength.
I ask for the strength to hold me strong;
I ask to live and see what growth is.

Let the butterflies come to my garden—
The gate is open, the sky is blue.
It's a heaven I can see whenever they do;
They relish the charm and sing.

Let the time bell be rung one time—
I shall respond to all, to all of a sudden.